AMANDA
NUNES

Amanda Nunes at UFC 269

AMANDA NUNES

ODYSSEYS

INDIRA MIDHA

CREATIVE EDUCATION · CREATIVE PAPERBACKS

Published by Creative Education and Creative Paperbacks
P.O. Box 227, Mankato, Minnesota 56002
Creative Education and Creative Paperbacks are imprints of
The Creative Company
www.thecreativecompany.us

Design and production by Blue Design (www.bluedes.com)
Art direction by Rita Marshall
Edited by Kremena Spengler

Images by Associated Press/Andrew Chin, cover; Dreamstime/Sergey Peterman, 22; Getty Images/Brandon Magnus, 4–5, Buda Mendes, 49, Carmen Mandato, 2, 54, 56–57, Chris Unger, 53, 63, Cooper Neill , 75, Handout, 42, Jeff Bottari, 6, 8–9, 17, 50, 66, 72–73, Josh Hedges, 29, 32–33, Josh Hedges/Forza LLC, 26–27, Vaughn Ridley, 68–69; Unsplash/Ole Kloth, 64; Wikimedia Commons/Andrius Petrucenia, 11, Bedois. bedois, 59, John Lamonica, 18, MMAnytt, 37, public domain, 24, Wilfredo Rafael Rodriguez Hernandez, 12–13

Library of Congress Cataloging-in-Publication Data
Names: Midha, Indira, author. Title: Amanda Nunes / by Indira Midha.
Description: Mankato, Minnesota : Creative Education and Creative Paperbacks, [2025] | Series: Odysseys in extreme sports | Includes bibliographical references and index. | Audience: Ages 12-15 years | Audience: Grades 7-9 | Summary: "Step into the Octagon with mixed martial arts (MMA) fighter Nunes. Witness triumphs, challenges, and risks in this extreme sports title for high school readers. Includes action photos, a glossary, index, and further resources"- Provided by publisher.
Identifiers: LCCN 2024030266 (print) | LCCN 2024030267 (ebook) | ISBN 9798889893158 (lib. bdg.) | ISBN 9781682776810 (paperback) | ISBN 9798889894261 (ebook)
Subjects: LCSH: Nunes, Amanda–Juvenile literature. | Mixed martial arts–Brazil–Pojuca–Biography–Juvenile literature.
Classification: LCC GV1102.7.M59 M54 2025 (print) | LCC GV1102.7.M59 (ebook) | DDC 796.81092 [B]–dc23/eng/20240812
LC record available at https://lccn.loc.gov/2024030266
LC ebook record available at https://lccn.loc.gov/2024030267

Printed in China

Amanda Nunes reacts to her victory over Miesha Tate at UFC 200.

Amanda Nunes strikes at Irene Aldana.

CONTENTS

UFC

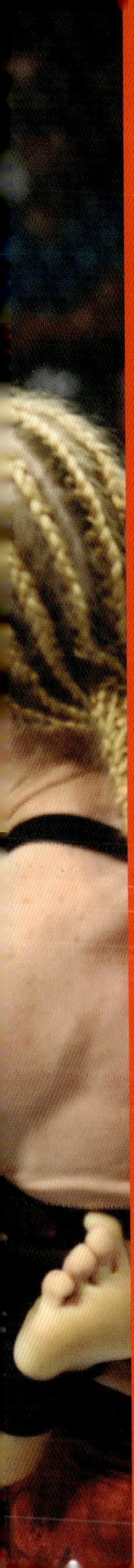

Introduction

Amanda Nunes stands as a towering figure in the world of women's mixed martial arts (MMA). Her skills and achievements have placed her name among the all-time greats of the sport. With a strong career marked by many title triumphs and record-breaking performances, Amanda has not only elevated her own status but has also played a pivotal role in shaping the world of MMA into what it is today.

OPPOSITE: Amanda Nunes kicks Valentina Shevchenko in the bantamweight fight at UFC 215 on September 9, 2017, in Edmonton, Alberta, Canada.

At its core, MMA is a combat sport that draws upon many fighting disciplines, including boxing, wrestling, judo, jujitsu, karate, Muay Thai (Thai boxing), and more. Competitors must master a varied blend of techniques, combining striking and grappling skills with strategic thinking and physical endurance.

Historically, MMA has been predominantly male-dominated, with men commanding the spotlight and honors in the sport. However, trailblazers like Amanda have broken barriers and paved the way for women to carve out their own legacies in this fiercely competitive arena. Through her talent, determination, and resilience, Amanda has not only claimed her place among the elite, but has also inspired many aspiring female athletes to pursue their dreams in and beyond the realm of MMA.

A championship belt

The Beginnings of a Trailblazer

Amanda Nunes was born on May 30, 1988, in Pojuca, a small town in the state of Bahia, Brazil. She grew up in a busy household with two older sisters, Valdirene and Vanessa. Life wasn't always easy for the Nunes family. Amanda's parents split up when she was just four years old, leaving her mother, Ivete, to raise her daughters alone. Despite the challenges, Ivete worked tirelessly, juggling multiple jobs, in addition to her role as an administrative assistant at a local school, to ensure her daughters had what they needed to be healthy, happy, and successful.

OPPOSITE: A view of Rio de Janeiro, Brazil

From a young age, Amanda was a ball of energy. She constantly sought outlets to channel her enthusiasm. Her mother recognized the importance of keeping Amanda engaged and enrolled her in various sports and other activities.

Amanda says her goal has always been to compete as a professional athlete, as she is passionate about sports as a whole. She ultimately chose to pursue MMA, but before she made that decision, she seriously had considered trying out for a professional Brazilian soccer team.

Amanda played in the striker position in soccer as a child. She excelled as a striker on several youth teams. Amanda went on to play on her hometown team and then on a team in Salvador, the capital of Bahia. She planned to try out for a more prestigious team when she started rethinking her future. As much as she enjoyed soccer,

Amanda was getting better at jiu-jitsu and decided to focus on just one sport in the hopes of achieving true mastery.

Amanda began her martial arts journey at age seven. She started with karate, discovering a passion for the discipline and self-expression that karate stood for. The turning point in Amanda's early years in martial arts came at the age of 16, when her sister Vanessa introduced her to Brazilian jiu-jitsu, a martial art practiced at the gym where Vanessa trained. It was there, amidst the sweat and camaraderie of the gym, that Amanda took her first steps into MMA. Though unfamiliar with the sport, Amanda dove in headfirst, fueled by a determination to conquer new challenges. With each training session, her skills sharpened, her resolve got stronger, and her dream of greatness burned ever brighter.

As Amanda immersed herself in MMA, she found herself craving greater challenges and opportunities for growth. The sport quickly became more than a hobby. It was a calling to Amanda—a path

Amanda Nunes weighs in before a fight on November 5, 2013, in Fort Campbell, Kentucky.

Brazilian Jiu-Jitsu

The name jiu-jitsu originated in Japan. In Japanese, the word Jū means "gentle," and the word Jutsu means "art." This combination makes jiu-jitsu "the gentle art." Jiu-jitsu is very popular in Brazil. The Brazilian form of the sport is a mostly ground-based martial art. It uses the knowledge of angles and an understanding of the human body to get a non-violent surrender from an opponent. Because of how much strategy goes into this martial art, it has been called "human chess." The sport is as mental as it is physical.

to self-discovery and empowerment. With every punch thrown and every submission mastered, she forged ahead, guided by the belief that she was destined for greatness. Little did she know that her journey was just beginning.

The city of Salvador called to Amanda with its promise of opportunity and growth. Leaving behind her hometown, she moved in with her sister Vanessa, who had already established herself in the bustling city. It was not long before Amanda found herself drawn to the Edson Carvalho Academy, known as the best place for Brazilian jiu-jitsu and judo training in the region. Under the guidance of Master Ricardo Carvalho, Amanda's journey towards greatness truly took off.

Days at the academy were grueling. Amanda spent hours honing her skills and pushing her limits both physically and mentally. The daily commute from Vanessa's home to the academy left Amanda exhausted and drained. She struggled to balance training with the demands of travel. Then Master Ricardo extended a generous offer—she could live at the gym. With nowhere else to turn, Amanda jumped at the chance, immersing herself fully into the world of martial arts.

Night after night, Amanda slept on the gym mat, her dreams mixed with the echoes of grueling training sessions from the day before. Each morning she rose alongside Master Ricardo before sunsrise, to prepare the academy for the day ahead. Surrounded by fellow athletes who shared her passion for the sports, Amanda found comfort in her newfound family. Yet, amidst the bonds forged in sweat and determination, Amanda often found herself the only woman among men—an all too familiar role she had grown accustomed to throughout her journey. MMA is a sport that is dominated by men to this day. It could have been intimidating, but Amanda set out on a mission to show women and girls around

MMA fighting requires intense training.

the world that they deserved a place in the sport, just as much as men did.

It was in the academy that Amanda earned her nickname—"The Lioness" or "Leoa" in Portuguese. She was the only woman among the pride of lions, and her resilience and ferocity shone through, earning her the admiration of her peers. The nickname served as a badge of honor, a testament to Amanda's spirit and tenacity in the face of adversity. Amanda was treated with great respect by Master Ricardo. But there were instances when she faced skepticism and disrespect

Judo

The Olympics define judo as a Japanese martial art that focuses on throws and other similar techniques to defeat opponents. It is similar to the martial art of jiu-jitsu because both are physically and mentally demanding sports. The main difference between the two sports is that judo is primarily practiced in standing positions while jiu-jitsu focuses on positions on the ground. Judo has been an Olympic sport since 1964 for men and 1992 for women. Jiu-jitsu is not an Olympic sport, and neither is MMA.

from her male peers, who believed MMA was not a sport where women belonged.

Under Master Ricardo's coaching, Amanda delved into the disciplines of jiu-jitsu and judo. These martial arts not only honed her physical skills, but also instilled in her a sense of versatility and adaptability—a hallmark of her fighting style.

Beyond the confines of the gym, Salvador's coastline offered her a chance for rest and reflection amidst the rhythmic lull of the sea. For Amanda, walks along the beach of Porto da Barra became a much-loved ritual, a moment of quiet amidst the chaos of her training. Though her days were consumed by the rigors of martial arts, the sea remained a constant source of inspiration, a reminder of the vastness of her dreams and the limitless potential that lay ahead.

MMA

Profession: Fighter

Amanda Nunes bravely entered the **cage** for her very first professional MMA fight in 2008, in Miami, Florida. She was 19 years old. The sport has no cutoff age to begin competing professionally, but most fighters, just like her, begin their careers in their late teens.

OPPOSITE: Amanda Nunes punches Alexis Davis during a Strikeforce fight on September 10, 2011, in Cincinnati, Ohio.

Amanda fought with determination and passion, eager to leave her mark on the sport. Initially, she competed in the featherweight division, where fighters must weigh 145 pounds (65.8 kilograms) or less. However, as Amanda's skills and confidence grew, she also ventured into the bantamweight class, which requires fighters to weigh 135 pounds (61.5 kg) or less. This transition allowed her to face a diverse group of opponents, further solidifying her reputation as a formidable and versatile force in the MMA world. She would later return to the featherweight class.

Amanda started her MMA career with an MMA organization called Prime MMA. She lost her first Prime MMA fight, but that did not discourage her. She won her next five fights—all by knockout (KO)!

In 2011, Amanda moved to Strikeforce, another MMA group. Her first fight with Strikeforce, against Julia Budd, was a very quick win for Amanda. The fight ended in just 14 seconds! But after an injury and a postponement, Amanda would lose her next fight with Strikeforce—against Alexis Davis—that September.

Amanda Nunes before a fight against Sheila Gaff

The following year, Amanda signed up with Invicta FC. She fought Raquel Pa'aluhi. Amanda won with a **rear naked choke** in round one. It was a dramatic match. Amanda landed some **leg kicks** early into the fight, but Pa'aluhi scored punches from the top. Amanda rebounded, and choked her opponent unconscious at the 2:24 mark (2 minutes and 24 seconds into the round).

Amanda's start with the Ultimate Fighting Championship (UFC)—perhaps the best known MMA organization in the world—was on August

3, 2013. The Lioness faced Sheila "The German Tank" Gaff at UFC 163 as a bantamweight. (The UFC numbers all its fights and fight nights, by placing the numbers after the letters UFC or after the event names.)

The Nunes–Gaff matchup took place in Brazil, Amanda's home country. Despite support from her Brazilian fans, Amanda had difficulty early on in the fight. However, she recovered, landing hard punches and elbows that dazed Gaff. As the referee resumed the fight, the women exchanged powerful punches. Gaff jumped on Amanda's back and pulled her down to the mat, but Amanda managed to hop back up. She took Gaff down, landing some powerful knee and elbow hits. The fight ended 2 minutes and 8 seconds after it started, with Amanda scoring a **technical knockout** (TKO).

Sheila Gaff punches Amanda Nunes in their bantamweight fight at UFC 163 on August 3, 2013, in Rio de Janeiro, Brazil.

BOOSTER
Fight Gear
UFC

Amanda would get her second UFC win at UFC Fight Night 31 in November 2013, with another first-round TKO. She quickly brought her opponent, Germaine "The Iron Lady" de Randamie, down to the mat, landing punches and elbow hits from above. De Randamie managed to block many of the hits, but after a fast final **barrage**, the referee stopped the fight.

Amanda was next named as the replacement for another fighter at an event called The Ultimate Fighter Nations Finale. But she ended up pulling out of the event because of an injury. She returned at UFC 178 in September 2014 but, despite a strong start, lost by TKO in round three to Cat Zingano.

However, Amanda scored impressive wins in her next three UFC events. At UFC Fight Night 62 in March 2015, she defeated Shayna "The Queen of Spades"

Baszlar with a TKO in round one. Baszlar had long been considered one of the strongest bantamweight fighters in the world.

Amanda next took on Sara McMann that August, at UFC Fight Night 73. An error in McMann's defense gave Amanda an early chance to land a right-hand hit, setting the tone for the fight. The end came at the 2:53 mark of round one, as Amanda administered a rear naked choke, forcing her opponent to **tap out**. The victory gave Amanda a $50,000 Performance of the Night bonus.

Facing Russian fighter Valentina Shevchenko the following March at UFC 196 in Las Vegas, Nevada, Amanda started out unexpectedly slowly. Both fighters worked hard and landed some hits. But Amanda had the advantage of strength. She manhandled her opponent, often holding the top position. Ultimately, the judges unanimously awarded her the win.

"This was a strong performance by Nunes, who showed the ability to pace herself for the first time in her career," wrote sports writer Andrew Richardson. "Normally, Nunes falls flat in fights that drag on past the opening frame, but this time she was dominant in the second and built up enough of a lead to ride out the victory... Following this win, Nunes is definitely up for a title shot."

After winning three fights in a row, Amanda got her chance to go for that title. On July 9, 2016, she challenged

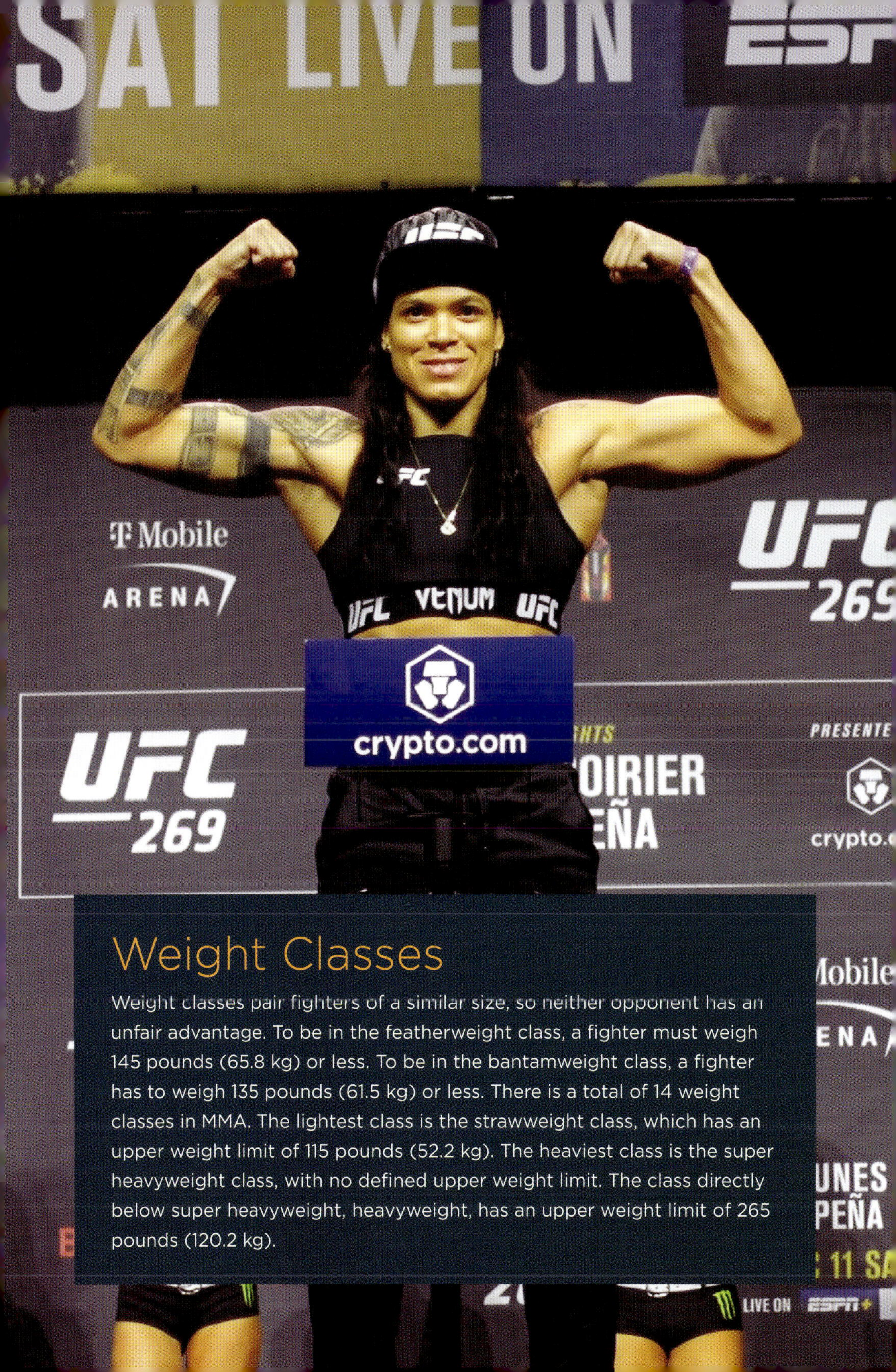

Weight Classes

Weight classes pair fighters of a similar size, so neither opponent has an unfair advantage. To be in the featherweight class, a fighter must weigh 145 pounds (65.8 kg) or less. To be in the bantamweight class, a fighter has to weigh 135 pounds (61.5 kg) or less. There is a total of 14 weight classes in MMA. The lightest class is the strawweight class, which has an upper weight limit of 115 pounds (52.2 kg). The heaviest class is the super heavyweight class, with no defined upper weight limit. The class directly below super heavyweight, heavyweight, has an upper weight limit of 265 pounds (120.2 kg).

then-bantamweight champion Miesha Tate at UFC 200 in Las Vegas. Amanda stunned her opponent early on with punches, one of which took Tate off her feet. Another right-hand hit dropped Tate down again and allowed Amanda to sink in a rear naked choke. She won by submission, 3 minutes and 16 seconds into round one.

"She's a very fast starter, very dangerous in the first round, and she caught me fair and square," Tate said of Amanda. "This is what I've been saying about Amanda; she's a very dangerous fighter, and I made some mistakes. I got careless, and it cost me really big."

On December 30, 2016, Amanda defended the bantameight title against Ronda Rousey at UFC 207. Amanda won by TKO, just 48 seconds into the fight. She next defended the title against Shevchenko at UFC 215 on September 9, 2017, winning by decision.

Amanda's next title defense was against Raquel Pennington at UFC 224 on May 12, 2018. Amanda won by TKO. The fight was noted as the first time two openly gay fighters had faced each other in the night's main event.

At UFC 323 on December 29, 2018, in Las Vegas, Amanda moved up a weight class. She challenged Cris "Cyborg" Justino for the featherweight title. In what was one of the most anticipated fights in UFC history, Amanda knocked out Justino just 51 seconds into the opening round.

The bout was very fast. The Lioness hit early with a right hand, after knocking Justino off balance with a leg kick. As Justino looked to move forward, Amanda dropped her to a knee with a right hand. Justino moved forward again, but Amanda dropped her to her knees with a left **hook**, then knocked her out with an **overhand** right.

The victory made 30-year-old Amanda the first female fighter to win, and concurrently hold, titles in two weight classes. According to UFC President Dana White, this accomplishment gave her a strong claim as the greatest female fighter of all time.

How Judges Decide the Winner

When an MMA bout goes on without a knockout or submission, the judges decide the winner by scoring each round. They use a 10-point system. The fighter who performs better receives 10 points, and the opponent receives nine or less. The scoring crietria include: effective striking, grappling, aggression, and **Octagon** control. Effective striking refers to clean, impactful punches, kicks, and knees that land on the opponent. Grappling includes **takedowns**, submission attempts, and controlling positions on the ground. Aggression measures a fighter's forward motion and intent to engage, while Octagon control assesses who sets the pace and location of the fight.

"She's the best ever," White said. "How can you deny it? That's what this fight was for. If you look at her résumé and who she's beat, she's the best ever. You can't debate that." The fight won Amanda another Performance of the Night award.

On July 6, 2019, Amanda defended the bantamweight title against Holly Holm in Las Vegas. This fight lasted 4 minutes and 10 seconds, and Amanda won by TKO.

On December 14, 2019, she faced a rematch for the bantamweight title with de Randamie. She outdid her opponent throughout this fight, and the judges declared her the winner.

Nunes vs. Spencer, 2020

The reigning two-division champion would also dominate in her featherweight title defense, at UFC 250 against Felicia Spencer on June 6, 2020. It would be her 11th win in a row.

MMA writer Damon Martin vividly described the featherweight title fight: "While she didn't fade away, Spencer was just outmatched on the feet as she continued to eat punches, with Nunes blasting her with thudding right hands again and again. With a smirk on her face almost the entire fight, Nunes continued walking Spencer down and then unleashing her powerful strikes."

Amanda defended the featherweight title again on March 6, 2021, at UFC 259, against Megan Anderson. Sports writers called this fight "a massive mismatch." The champion started out by firing off a kick, then rocked the challenger with a right hand. Anderson wobbled and answered with a **spinning back fist**, but it fell short. The Lioness went for a takedown, locking in a triangle **arm bar**. Anderson tapped out 2 minutes and 3 seconds after the bout began.

Amanda would defend her bantamweight title yet again at UFC 269 on December 11, 2021. Her opponent was Julianna Peña. The Lioness dominated the first round but was outstruck during the second. She lost the title, submitting after a rear naked choke.

But she bounced back in a rematch with Peña at UFC 277 on July 30, 2022. She won the title back af-

“AMANDA BECAME THE FIRST PERSON IN UFC HISTORY TO BECOME A DOUBLE CHAMPION TWICE.”

ter five rounds, on a unanimous judges’ decision. As a result, Amanda became the first person in UFC history to become a double champion twice. A third rematch with Peña was postponed after Peña suffered an injury.

In her last fight before retirement, the Lioness faced Irene Aldana at UFC 289 in June 2023. Despite being 35 years old, both fighters exhibited remarkable skill and determination, going the full five rounds. Amanda emerged victorious, earning a unanimous decision from the judges.

Rivalries and Impact

Ranked the number-one female fighter at the time of the time of her retirement, Amanda Nunes holds many UFC records. They include her two bantamweight and one featherweight titles; the record for most wins in title fights among women (11); and eight successful title defenses. She holds the distinction of being the first and only woman to achieve double-champion status in the UFC.

Amanda is the first fighter in the UFC, man or woman, to defend titles in two divisions while holding them both. She is also the only UFC fighter to retire as a two-division champion. She has won five Performance of the Night awards in different fights and many cash prizes.

Amanda exemplifies the resilience and skill required to succeed in MMA. The sportsmanship and respect she exhibits are in line with the core values of MMA. With an impressive record of 23 wins and five losses in 28 professional fights with the UFC, including 13 victories by knockout, her skill in the Octagon is undeniable. Her accomplishments not only showed her talent and determination but also inspired many in the sport, breaking barriers and setting new standards for female athletes in mixed martial arts.

Even the greatest fighters experience injury, and Amanda is no exception. She faced significant challenges in her UFC bantamweight title loss to Peña in 2021, citing double knee injuries that affected her performance. The Lioness revealed that she struggled with knee issues

Striker Style

Amanda Nunes is known as a striker—a fighter who utilizes various parts of the body as weapons. Strikers use stand-up techniques to dominate opponents on the feet. They excel in boxing, kickboxing, Muay Thai, and traditional karate, relying on precise strikes delivered with speed and power. Central to their strategy is maintaining distance, to take advantage of their superior striking range. They evade takedowns to keep the fight standing. Strikers are skilled at employing jabs, crosses, hooks, and kicks, often blending them into combinations that can quickly overwhelm opponents. Footwork and timing are critical, enabling strikers to maneuver around the Octagon efficiently and strike when they see an opportunity.

Nunes takes a hit in the 2021 match against Peña.

leading up to the fight, limiting her ability to train and perform at her usual level. Despite being one of MMA's most dominant fighters, Amanda admitted that the injuries decreased her mobility and affected her preparation. This setback underscores the physical demands and risks fighters like Amanda face, even at the height of their careers. It highlights the importance of injury management and recovery in the rigorous world of MMA.

Her rivalry with Peña has also captured the attention of fans worldwide. Their intense matchups have shown the unpredictable nature of MMA, adding to the sport's excitement and drama.

The rivalry between Amanda and Peña in MMA heated up before their title fight in 2021. Peña, known for her outspokenness and confidence, challenged Amanda in the bantamweight championship. Peña criticized Amanda's dominance and claimed she was ready to dethrone the reigning champion. The Lioness, on the other hand, defended her legacy as one of the best fighters in the sport, confident in her skills despite Peña's verbal jabs. Their clash in the Octagon was highly anticipated, with fans eager to see if Peña could upset Amanda's impressive winning streak.

Leading up to their fight, tensions rose during press conferences and interviews, as both fighters exchanged verbal barbs. Peña aimed to take advantage of Amanda's perceived weaknesses, while Amanda remained focused on maintaining her championship status. Their rivalry highlighted the competitive nature of MMA, showing the intensity and determination that fighters like them bring to the sport.

Amanda's head was not solely in the Octagon anymore

Amanda Nunes makes a comeback against Julianna Peña in the bantamweight championship fight at UFC 277 on July 30, 2022, in Dallas, Texas.

Amanda Nunes celebrates after defeating Julianna Peña in the bantamweight championship fight.

after these fights, especially after becoming a mother. Her decision to retire at the peak of her career surprised many. But it was a result of her desire to put her family first and to allow her body to heal and rest after years of intense training. Many of her fans were shocked and disappointed, but many were supportive of her choice.

As Amanda began a new chapter of her life, her journey in MMA serves as a testament to the power of perseverance and the importance of following one's dreams. While she may no longer compete in the Octagon, Amanda's influence on the sport will endure, leaving a mark on the world of MMA for years to come.

NUNES
VS PEÑA
UFC

The Power of Identity

Amanda Nunes has held her Brazilian heritage close to her heart. Her upbringing was shaped by the culture and traditions of her homeland. However, her journey to becoming one of the most formidable fighters in the world took her far from her roots.

OPPOSITE: Amanda Nunes holds her daughter Raegan on stage at UFC 269.

“THROUGHOUT HER CAREER, AMANDA HAS NEVER FORGOTTEN HER ROOTS.”

In pursuit of greater opportunities in her fighting career, Amanda made the bold decision to move to U.S. in 2007. She believed that her chances for growth and success were greater in the U.S. than in Brazil, a decision that would prove to be pivotal in her career. Amanda's move to the U.S. opened doors to a world of possibilities.

However, Amanda's transition to life in the U.S. was not without its challenges. As she rose through the ranks of MMA, she faced criticism from some Brazilian fans who believed she should have remained in Brazil.

The emblem of Pojuca, Amanda Nunes's hometown

On social media, opinions about Amanda varied widely, from both critics and fans. Yet, despite the occasional backlash, she remained steadfast in her commitment to both her craft and to her Brazilian identity.

Throughout her career, Amanda has never forgotten her roots. Despite competing on an international stage, she has always proudly represented her homeland, embodying the spirit and resilience of Brazilian fighters. When she returns to Brazil, she is greeted with overwhelming love and admiration from her fans, a testament to the pride they feel in her accomplishments.

As she announced her retirement from MMA, Amanda issued a challenge to fellow Brazilian fighters, urging them to pursue UFC titles and carry on the legacy of excellence in the sport. Her call to action reflects her desire to inspire the next generation of Brazilian athletes, encouraging them to reach for greatness.

In addition to her achievements in the sport, Amanda made history as the first openly gay champion in the UFC. Embracing this milestone, she became a vocal advocate for LGBTQIA+ rights. Amanda's advocacy extends beyond sports, reflecting her commitment to promoting inclusion and acceptance in society at large. She is an admired figure in the LGBTQIA+ community around the globe.

Amanda' journey in love and family is as remarkable as her achievements in the MMA Octagon. It began when she crossed paths with Nina Ansaroff, a U.S. strawweight fighter, in 2012, during **sparring** sessions in Florida. Their connection flourished and ultimately turned into a relationship, marking them as the first openly lesbian couple in UFC history. In 2018, they took a significant step forward by getting engaged. They exchanged vows the following year, officially becoming Amanda and Nina Nunes.

Their love story deepened with the arrival of their daughters. The couple welcomed their first daughter, Raegan Ann Nunes, in 2020. Their second daughter, Hazel Ann Nunes, was born in 2023.

The Nunes family has become a symbol of success

and resilience in the LGBTQIA+ community, celebrated for their accomplishments both inside and outside MMA. In 2021, ESPN invited the couple to participate in a question-and-answer session during LGBTQIA+ Pride Month. Amanda and Nina shared their experiences and offered support to those grappling with their coming-out process, encouraging them to seek assistance. Amanda's willingness to be a listening ear for those in need underscores her compassion, extending beyond her athletic achievements.

Amanda's journey to self-acceptance was not easy, despite knowing her truth about her identity from a young age. Raised in a traditional small-town Brazilian family, she grappled with fear and uncertainty about her family's reaction to her sexuality. Ultimately, it was one of Amanda's sisters who took the initiative to disclose her

Amanda and her wife Nina

Rainbow flags represent the LGBTQIA+ community.

sexual orientation to their mother, relieving Amanda of the burden. Her loved ones were ultimately supportive of her and glad that she was able to live as her true self.

Motherhood has added a new layer of pride and joy to Amanda's life, which she shares openly on social media. From sporting accessories with her daughter Raegan's name during fights to celebrating victories with Raegan by her side in the cage prior to her retirement, Amanda embraced every side of motherhood with enthusiasm and affection. Raegan, and later Hazel, who was born after Amanda's retirement, have served as her biggest motivator and source of happiness.

Amanda's impact extends beyond the Octagon, reaching into the hearts of fans worldwide. Her journey as an openly lesbian athlete has inspired individuals to embrace their true selves and pursue their dreams

Amanda Nunes celebrates a win with daughter Raegan.

without fear of judgment or discrimination. Through her advocacy and visibility, Amanda has helped to break down barriers and create a more inclusive and accepting world for LGBTQIA+ individuals in sports and beyond.

As Amanda continues to navigate the complexities of love, family, and career, one thing remains constant:

"AMANDA HAS HELPED TO BREAK DOWN BARRIERS AND CREATE A MORE INCLUSIVE AND ACCEPTING WORLD FOR LGBTQIA+ INDIVIDUALS IN SPORTS AND BEYOND."

her commitment to living fearlessly. Whether she's inside the Octagon or advocating for LGBTQIA+ rights, Amanda's presence serves as a reminder that strength comes in many forms and that love is a powerful force for change.

What's Next for Amanda?

Amanda and Nina Nunes have settled into life in Florida with their daughters, enjoying parenthood. In an interview, Amanda opened up about her decision to step away from MMA, explaining that she is taking some time off to focus on her children—and savoring every moment of it.

OPPOSITE: Retired Amanda Nunes looks on during a bantamweight title fight between Raquel Pennington and Mayra Bueno Silva at UFC 297.

Fighting has been a central part of her adult life, leaving little room for the leisurely experiences that most people enjoy in their twenties, she explained. Yet she looks back on her journey with gratitude, recognizing that every challenge and sacrifice has shaped her into the person and athlete she is today. Amanda finds joy in her marriage and motherhood, cherishing the opportunity to embrace new roles and experiences.

However, amidst the serenity of family life, one question continues to linger: when will Amanda return to the Octagon? While fans eagerly await her comeback, Amanda's response remains elusive, leaving room for speculation.

Amanda's passion for the sport is undeniable. Yet, she also values the chance to step back from the rigorous training **regimen** and enjoy the comforts of home.

Balancing the demands of her career with the desire for a more relaxed lifestyle presents a unique challenge for Amanda, who acknowledges the difficulty of maintaining the relentless discipline required of a fighter.

Despite the allure of leisurely days spent at home, Amanda's competitive spirit still burns bright. The thrill of stepping into the cage, the **adrenaline** rush of victory—it's a part of who she is. And while she may be savoring this time away from the gym, Amanda knows that her love for the sport will inevitably draw her back into the fray.

Despite Amanda's retirement from MMA, her influence on the sport persists. While she may no longer be competing, she maintains the strength, intelligence, and mindset that defined her championship career. She continues to embody the qualities of a true champion, inspiring fans worldwide.

How Much Does a Fighter Make?

Amanda has amassed a significant amount of money from her MMA career. As of UFC 289, her earnings had reached an impressive $2,428,500. That's a pretty penny! This substantial sum reflects her success and skill in the sport. It is clear that Amanda's dedication and hard work have paid off, both in terms of victories in the Octagon and financial rewards. With such earnings, she has undoubtedly secured her place among the top earners in the world of MMA.

UFC
crypto.com

Despite stepping away from active competition, Amanda remains an influential figure in the MMA community. Her words and actions continue to matter to fans, serving as a source of inspiration and empowerment. Whether advocating for LGBTQIA+ rights or sharing insights into her life as a mother and spouse, Amanda's presence is felt far beyond the confines of the Octagon.

While the future may hold uncertainties, one thing is certain: Amanda Nunes will forever be remembered as one of the sport's greatest champions. Her contributions to MMA have left an enduring legacy, inspiring generations of athletes to strive for greatness. As fans eagerly await her next move, Amanda's impact on the sport will continue to be felt for years to come.

Amanda Nunes poses for a portrait after UFC 289 on June 10, 2023, in Vancouver, Canada.

Selected Bibliography

Aiddo, Clyde. "Amanda Nunes Recounts Experience Coming out, Offers To Help Others." MMA News, June 27, 2021. https://www.mmanews.com/news/amanda-nunes-recounts-experience-coming-out-offers-to-help-others.

Mahjouri, Shakiel. "UFC 289 Results, Highlights: Amanda Nunes Announces Sudden Retirement after Dominant Win over Irene Aldana." CBSSports.com, June 11, 2023. https://www.cbssports.com/mma/news/ufc-289-results-highlights-amanda-nunes-announces-sudden-retirement-after-dominant-win-over-irene-aldana/live/.

Martin, Damon. "Amanda Nunes Hints at Potential Comeback: 'I Still Feel like a Champion, so We'll See.'" MMA Fighting, January 21, 2024. https://www.mmafighting.com/2024/1/21/24045711/amanda-nunes-hints-at-potential-comeback-i-still-feel-like-a-champion-so-well-see.

Glossary

adrenaline a hormone that helps a person react quickly in a dangerous, stressful, or exiting situation

arm bar a move in which a fighter straightens an opponent's arm out, then forces it beyond its normal range at the elbow

barrage a large amount of something that comes all at the same time

cage the place where an MMA fight takes place

hook the use of careful positioning of feet and legs to control the movement or the position of an opponent

leg kick kick typically targeting an opponent's calf, thigh, or knee area

LGBTQIA+ the letters stand for "lesbian," "gay," "bisexual," "transgender," "queer," "intersex," and "asexual"; the + sign stands for "other"

Octagon the eight-sided raised platform surrounded by fencing that is used for UFC fights. The angles are wider than a square, preventing fighters from getting trapped.

overhand a punch thrown with the back of the hand

rear naked choke a chokehold applied from an opponent's back

regimen a regular course of exercise and/or diet to promote health

sparring a practice session in combat sports in which athletes engage in simulated fights or drills with training partners

spinning back fist a punch thrown with the back of the fist at the end of a quick spinning motion

submission the act of securing a hold on an opponent that causes them to tap out as a result of the pain and discomfort

takedown the act of pulling an opponent to the ground to gain an advantage

tap out to signal defeat by tapping on the floor or on a part of the opponent's body

technical knockout (TKO) when a referee calls an end to a fight because one of the fighters is no longer able to defend themselves

Websites

Mixed Martial Arts (MMA)
UFC, Fighting Styles, Boxing, Techniques...
https://www.britannica.com/sports/mixed-martial-arts
Learn more about the sport of MMA.

Amanda Nunes (Women's Bantamweight)
MMA Profile - ESPN
https://www.espn.com/mma/fighter/_/id/2516131/amanda-nunes
Check out Amanda's career stats.

What Are the Different MMA Fighting Styles in the UFC?
https://tfcgym.com.au/mma-fighting-styles/
Learn more about different fighting styles.

Index